Thanks Inky

Tales of a police dog handler

DAVID DAVIES

authorHOUSE®

AuthorHouse™ UK Ltd.
500 Avebury Boulevard
Central Milton Keynes, MK9 2BE
www.authorhouse.co.uk
Phone: 08001974150

First published by AuthorHouse 6/5/2007

ISBN: 978-1-4259-9657-4 (sc)

Printed in the United States of America
Bloomington, Indiana

This book is printed on acid-free paper.

Index

Preface

The author has been a police officer in Britain for over 26 years, and over half of that time he has served as a dog handler. During this period he has trained and handled numerous German shepherd dogs, trained as General Purpose dogs. These types of dogs are used for detaining suspects, tracking, searching, and a host of other skills. The author has also trained and handled dogs able to search for narcotics, and firearms.

Unconnected with the police service the author runs a successful dog training business, (www.happydogsnortheast.co.uk), which was originally used as a learning curve to acquire knowledge on various breeds of dogs, (their owners), and breed specific behaviours.

The authors interest in becoming a police dog handler started as a child, when he was heavily influenced by the character depicted as PC Snow,

with his police dog Inky in the TV drama, 'Z-Cars,'
It is thanks to that character that this book is now
being printed!

Please note that although these tales are from
real life encounters, all names and places are
fictitious.

1 Max & the wheelbarrow

Stand still, I shouted at the top of my voice. Stand still or I will release the dog. Police Dog Max, A big woolly grey haired German shepherd came flying from the quick release hatch in the dog cage in the Astramax Van. Off he went in hot pursuit of a tall lanky youth in his early twenties who was running as fast as his long legs would carry him.

I had responded to a call on the police radio to a theft from an elderly gentleman's garden shed. A tall lanky man had been seen by the gentleman to break into his garden shed and steal his lawn mower. The thief had also stolen his wheelbarrow, loaded the lawnmower into it and pushed it off down the street.

I tried to think the most likely area the thief would head for, and how far he could have travelled on foot pushing a wheelbarrow. In this case I had been right. There he was. It was about 4am. No one else around, it had to be him. I pulled up in my police dog van expecting him to run away. He didn't. Infact he put the wheelbarrow down and walked up to me. I alighted from the van and spoke to the lad, introducing myself. Without warning (although a cop should always be on his guard), the lad threw a handful of coins into my face. I managed to shield my eyes, but it caused a couple of seconds delay. Enough for him to turn and run. He was very tall. I am 5'11" he towered above me. His great legs covering huge amounts of ground as he ran. I was never going to get near him. I didn't need to. I had 80LBS of German shepherd dog in the form of Max in the van. I quickly opened the drivers' door on the van. The quick exit hatch on the dog cage was already open. I didn't need to tell Max, he had heard everything. He was whining and scratching at the mesh on the cage wanting to do his bit. Out he came, wisps of fine soft hair blowing in the air as he went. He had lovely soft hair; I have never known a GSD with such a soft coat. It did use to get up ones nose and irritate it though.

I called out the challenge into the night air. I am sure Max though it most unsporting of me, but one has to give running criminals a chance to avoid the 42 teeth of a police dog, and if they comply it makes a lot less paperwork for me!

It made no difference. Not even a backward glance. Very silly though. Had he made for a fence to climb or even a garden, but he just ran along the open footpath. I ran after them in full knowledge that this person was in the bag. Max was very experienced at this game, he would not fail. Grrrowl I heard. Max always made that sound just before he sank his teeth into any wrongdoers flesh. A blood-curdling scream emitted from the mouth of the running criminal. A dull thud as he hit the hard pavement. Max had hold of this lad's right arm, and he wasn't going to let go. The lad screamed and thrashed about. As I caught up to the heap on the footpath I saw him kick Max with his foot. An understandable reaction, but very ill advised. Max held on relentlessly and began shaking this individual like a terrier with a rat. I must admit to feeling sorry for this lad. When a dog shakes like that, its teeth dig deeper and deeper into flesh. I knew he was going to have some very deep puncture wounds. Also, a bite is a crush injury, so once the dog releases and all the blood rushes back into the site of the bite the wound becomes very painful.

Stand still, I instructed "LEAVE", "Max, LEEEAVE" Max spat the arm out of his mouth stepped back about 1 meter and began barking, keeping this person under surveillance, as trained.

David Davies

"Do exactly what I tell you and you will come to no more harm," I instructed my prisoner. "I am arresting you on suspicion of theft, & assault on police," I then cautioned him (read him his rights). His reply to caution was "I didn't think police dogs were allowed to bite people." He now knows differently! I walked him back to the wheelbarrow and lawn mower and awaited a police van to transport the stolen property and the lad to the local police custody office.

2 Max and the river bank

It was a pleasant sunny summers evening. I was piloting the little Astramax Dog van around villages local to my home. I heard a vehicle pursuit come over the radio. It was a Panda car crewed by local officers whom I knew well. They had been suspicious of a vehicle being driven in front of them. As they had illuminated the blue roof light on their police vehicle, the suspicious car, occupied by two men sped off from them. As a dog handler, whenever there is a pursuit one should always be trying to pre-empt where the vehicle being followed may go, otherwise one is always heading for the last location given which is really no use whatsoever. This sort of knowledge comes from years of working certain areas, and knowing whom the suspects are likely to be and where the best-perceived escape routs are for the criminals. I was now playing catch up. Then I overheard the officers say the vehicle had been lost. When this happens anyone involved and not reassigned to a new detail should head for likely areas and wait in the hope one may catch a glimpse of the vehicle.

Several minutes, probably over half an hour had passed when the same panda car crew called up stating they had found the vehicle abandoned. There was no sign of anyone with the car. It had been located in a country area between two small villages and close to open countryside leading to a large, wide river bordering two counties. The officers requested that a dog unit be deployed. I responded by stating I was five minutes away.

On arriving at the location I was greeted by two young constables whom explained fully what had taken place, and the fact that this was confirmed as a stolen vehicle. It was now time for me to do my bit, the bit I have always loved. I went to the rear doors of the dog van and opened them up. There was dear old Max looking out of the cage at me with eagerness in his beautiful eyes, his great thick bush of a grey tail swishing from side to side. Max was the first police dog I handled. He was a big grey coloured dog, long coated. He had a very laid-back nature, almost to a point of laziness. Until he was chasing some wrong doer, then he came alive. Come on son I said to him as I opened the cage and he jumped out looking up at me with anticipation. I removed all the paraphernalia I required for the impending search, tracking harness, 30' tracking line, slip chain, leash, hand held radio, etc. etc. "Head" I said to him, asking him to place his great woolly head into the loop of the check chain so as to keep him safe in his eagerness by the roadside. He obliged accordingly and assisted me in scanning the field to our left side for a glimpse of evidence as to where the two lads may have headed. There was no clue, but the field to the left seemed the most likely place they would initially head for. There was nothing else to do except cast Max around the stolen car to try to ascertain the direction these lads had taken. I asked the two police officers whom had initiated the job to go in opposite directions along the road and to stop any vehicles or pedestrians so I could task Max with searching for scent of the lads. Once done, I placed Max in the leather tracking harness. This harness is used so as the dog can work safely on a leash or line, but not be impeded as it may be if worked from a collar. Max circled the stolen car sniffing the ground enthusiastically. He knew that a successful location of a scent can very often lead to finding the bad guys and if they run he can chase them and get hold of them. He loved that bit.

One always knows when the dog has located a likely scent on the ground. It sniffs around, and then suddenly flicks its head back to the bit it thought was of interest, checks it again, and then in the case of Max gives a big body shake. I never knew if this was excitement or maybe shaking off excess scent from himself so as not to interfere with his olfactory system when following the trail!

He always did this and it was a good clue to me that we were onto something.

Not letting me down he soon did all these actions and off we went. Tracks are always a bit hit and miss in the first stages. The dog has to be convinced it is on the right trail, as does the handler. Hours can be wasted by following the wrong person. Usually an over enthusiastic cop who has been waiting for the dog team to arrive, and had a walk about, although they always assure you that they haven't been anywhere!!! Very annoying.

We set off into the field following a route diagonally across it and into the back garden of a lone bungalow. There the owner came out very indignant that we had gone into his garden. I explained the reason and that I was sure the people we were hunting had gone that way. The man (whom I knew, I lived not far from this place), took great delight as often people sadly seem to do, in trying to dash my confidence by pointing out no one had been there and police dogs were never any use! I continued on. I trusted Max and knew well his ability. I asked the man to leave us alone as Max was now becoming suspicious of his intentions as he was shouting. Max was quite adept at dealing with people whom he believed to be threatening me, and I didn't want this to turn into one of those occasions! Once this chap had gone back into his house, I said calmly "seek on son, seek on," with this Max set too with his bulberous black nose, searching for the trail that in the excitement he had momentarily lost. Bang we were back on. Not been in his garden HUH! Max stood still looking at me then at the ground swishing his tail. A balaclava still warm to touch lay beneath a barbed wire fence leading from Mr. Angrys garden to a steep bank leading down to The River. I called this in on my radio asking for one of the cops to recover it as it was evidence and I had more than enough to carry. Now I knew we were right. That boost to ones confidence is immeasurable. We set off at speed down a steep bank. As usual I fell over and beat Max to the riverbank, crashing into debris on the way in the form of tree trunks. I lay there for a moment checking to see if I had broken any bones. Max just continued undaunted by my theatrical performance, which he was quite accustomed to. I had dropped the leash in my efforts to grab hold of something on the way down. As the loop in the end of the 30' leash slid past me, I took hold of it and continued on behind Max. The riverbank was overgrown. The river was very wide, rust coloured and was full, it had obviously recently been in flood. I knew the river well and realised the current would be dangerous should these lads try to cross it. As we continued, Max would from time to time go to the waters edge. I could see when he did this signs of disturbance to the bank side. Obviously, the two lads were considering crossing over the river, but each time Max would continue on. We approached a static caravan park. There walking towards me was a family. I quickly enquired if they had seen anyone. Joy of joys. They had, and they went on to describe two young men in their late teens early twenties whom had been running frantically through the undergrowth. Max now had to sort out the scent of the suspects with that of the family, but he soon did this and off we went. About ten minutes went by from meeting the family when Max started to pull very hard. This usually means the scent has become fresher. Perhaps the two lads had slowed down or taken a rest, then set off again. I then saw Max change from ground scent to air scent. This can be due to a change in wind direction if the scent starts to blow towards the dog. I checked there was no discernable wind and what breeze there was went with the flow of the river (the same direction we were moving in). We were getting close. Then a bark from Max, just one high-pitched bark of excitement and he dragged me towards a pile of tree trunks washed up by the recently flooded river. I then heard a crashing sound and a shout. Two young men broke from the cover of the tree stumps and ran for the river. Fully clothed they jumped in. The current grabbed them and started washing them quickly down stream. I called out to them, but they could not hear me. Not that they would have stopped. I recognised them both. They were prolific car thieves and small time drug dealers. To their credit they were good swimmers. They didn't panic, just went with the current and swam across the river. I ran down the bank side requesting assistance, and asking as I had already done for the neighbouring force to be alerted and despatch an officer or two. The excitement was all too much for Max. He could not understand why I wasn't in hot pursuit and directing him to chase. Within a flash he had heroically plunged into the swollen river and with 30' of trailing line following he swam after these two. After all this work they are not getting away, he must have thought! I tried to call him back. I didn't want to have to place myself at risk of drowning, I certainly didn't want to risk Max, and the 30' line was highly likely to become fouled on the other bank side. Max however was focused, and probably couldn't hear me due to the river. I tried to go in, but weighed down by all the equipment I was unable do so whatsoever. I stood up to my chest in water and watched in horror as brave Max crossed the river in pursuit of these two offenders. The other side of the river at this point is a very very steep bank, highly overgrown in summer, and heavily wooded. Max was still crossing the river when I saw the two lads crawl out onto the opposite bank side in safety. They ran at the steep wooded area, but soon there legs were helpless. One lad climbed a tree, the other scrambled at the bank side trying to run along side the riverbank. I watched in horror as Max pulled himself out of the river and went for the lad by the riverside. This lad stood still upon seeing Max. I prayed the line on Max would not snag and that these two did not hurt him. Max was very capable, but against two with a plentiful supply of heavy branches he would be unlikely to be the victor.

The lad froze to the spot. Max barked at him. I then saw the other youth in the tree begin to climb down. Max must have heard him because he turned, and ran at the tree making the most awful din I ever heard him make. Somehow the line did not snag on anything. Max continued bouncing between the two lads in this way for some time while I tried to decide how to deal with the situation. This area is a very rural spot. I knew assistance was coming but it had to be by foot, and we must have been several miles from any road. Air support was then a vision for the future for a county force like ours!

It was now that all the obedience training one does with their dog paid off. Many dog owners and professional handlers scoff at the amount of obedience work that is suggested we do with our dogs. Well what follows shows how important this can be. A lifesaver! I called on Max to lie down and stay. He did, even though he was about one hundred and fifty yards across a river from me. With two lads he was intent on detaining. I then instructed the two lads that if they felt able to safely swim back over to me, to do so. I was amazed, they obliged. Once they were half way across the river to me, I recalled Max, whom swam back. Now these two lads are baddies. As I said, I knew them. For some minutes, I was alone with them until Max joined us. They however were so amazed (as was I), at Max's skill all they did was sing his praises.

I formally arrested and cautioned them both and escorted them along the riverbank to the caravan park, where a police car was waiting. A lone officer concerned for my safety red in the face and sweating profusely met us on route. On seeing whom we had arrested he made comment as to why I hadn't let the dog bite them. I said, why, they have done exactly what I asked of them and given me no problems. They did not try to hurt Max as even though they could have won they would have been hurt. I knew I would come up against these two again, as I had done previously. If my reputation were that I would set the dog on people for no just reason, apart from it being illegal, then the suspects would have nothing to lose by trying to injure the dog. I have never and would never badly use a police dog. It is not fair on the dog, unfair on the individual if they are complying, and my reputation means more to me than anything.

We escorted the two to the waiting police car and they were driven to the local town police custody office. They were charged with the offence of theft of the vehicle and several other offences they were wanted for. At court Max's heroic efforts were commended, he also went on to get an award for his abilities from The Forces Chief Constable.

This benevolent attitude shown to the two lads when arrested was to pay off when I met these two again on a later occasion.

3 The Engagement ring

Driving my little van through a small village late one night, (most of dog sections successes are on a night duty). I came across a young couple, they seemed distressed. Now I have never liked interfering with peoples private business. As cops, we are encouraged to and some times it is necessary, but I do feel we can make matters worse by doing it. Anyhow, I observed for a moment to make sure no one was in any danger. The young lady was sobbing. They seemed to be looking at the ground as if they had lost something. I alighted from the van. Resisting the urge to say "Evening All," I enquired if I could help them. They were a lovely young couple. They said they had been arguing, and the lady said she pulled her engagement ring off and in a temper threw it away. I tried to calm her down, she was distraught. I went to the van to get a torch. I don't know why. Police torches never work. There was a glimmer of light from it, but it wasn't much use.

A loud wine from the back of the van reminded me I had a large dog in the back with a wonderful olfactory system, trained especially for times such as these! To be truthful I really didn't think a small engagement ring on a roadside would hold much scent for a dog to find. I decided it would at least look like I cared (which I did), so I made the usual investigative questions to ascertain if I thought the boy could do it.

How many people have walked over the area, how long since the ring was lost. Etc, etc. It transpired only they had walked over the area, and it was only ten minutes since the lady had pulled it from her finger.

I brought Max from the van. The ladies always loved Max. This was no exception. She stroked his huge soft head and spoke to him. Dogs are so soothing. Anyone who suffers stress should have access to a soft-coated dog. As one strokes it one can feel the stress leaving.

I sat him down wind of where the couple stated the ring should be. Seeko I said quietly to Max. Sniff sniff he went, his black nose clicking away. When a dog scents its nose can sound like a rattle. He traversed back and forth, fully focussed upon his task. The couple watched on in anticipation. I had never asked Max to look for anything this small before, and comprised of metal, not withstanding it to be precious metal and precious stones, I really didn't hold out much hope.

Max trotted out to the centre of the road. He sniffed the ground, moved on then flicked his head back. He stood for a moment, and then looked as if he was trying to pick something up. He trotted back to me sat down and looked at me. I didn't dare say anything; I didn't want to build the couples hopes up to find he had brought me an old fag butt or something. I cupped my hands and held them out under his mouth. Plonk, he dropped an engagement ring into my hand. Is this what you are looking for I enquired smugly, trying to look confident that I knew this would be the result. Oh yes they said, relieved.

The lady hugged Max. I had to make do with a handshake from her fiancé. Max as usual swished his tail. I popped him back in his cage, and drove off. I felt so good. Not smug because of finding the ring. I felt GOOD. You see, the nature of police work means that even if one party is pleased with what you do for them, there is usually a second party whom hates you with a passion. This was one of those rare occasions where one manages to please everyone. It's lovely.

4 Never kiss a dog; you don't know where it's been!

Most of what I have thus far written has been about General Purpose, or Patrol Dogs. These are typically German Shepherds, but other breeds are considered. It is not the breed of dog that matters as much as its abilities.

In the police service we also handle dogs for what we term specialist duties. These are typically drugs or explosive detection dogs. Again any breed will be considered, but one usually can expect to see Labrador retrievers or Springer Spaniels trained for the task.

I myself handled a black Labrador, named Mikey. He was narcotics and firearm detection trained. Mikey was a timid little lad when I acquired him. He had been trained as a gun dog.

The training in this field is typically hard and if the dog is of a delicate disposition it is unfair for anyone to continue with a dog such as this. Mikey was such a dog. His trainer became disillusioned with him because he would not jump dry stonewalls on the fells, and would run home when the trainer raised his voice at him.

I took Mikey home, more because I felt sorry for him rather than I believed he would make a good police search dog. I have always been soft like that, but I have always been repaid tenfold!

I remember putting him in the bath at home. He was smelly, covered in fleabites, and frightened of everything. (I should mention he is still with me, fat old, and very loved. As with the majority of my dogs I asked to keep him when he retired).

This was a typical request for assistance with a narcotics search. I was requested by CID to search a small council house. The owner had been arrested for supplying Heroin. He and his family were at the house when I arrived. It took me a while to get there as I had to travel the length of the entire county to get there. On my arrival there was a lot of shouting taking place. The family did not understandably want the police there and were very hostile to them. However I went in identified myself to all present. I then went to the van and brought Mikey back into the house with me. It always amazed me. I could turn up at a detail, in full dog section uniform. The people whose house I was to search would be remonstrating with the police officers already there, I would turn up and they would be totally civil to me, to a point of giving the dog a drink of water if he needed it.

I went up stairs into the bedrooms with Mikey, followed by a very smart CID officer dressed in a suit, and the householder. I must have resembled a womble, covered in Shepherd hair having just cleaned out the van.

"Hash," I said to Mikey. This was the command I used for him to search for drugs. Off he went. It wasn't long before he indicated on the floorboards in the main bedroom. Mikey was trained to give a passive indication. Once over we used what's called an active indication. The dog would scratch to identify where the scent of the drug was emanating from. We trained this by hiding the dogs' toy with the narcotic and the dog learned that by digging at the source of the scent it would find its toy. The trouble with this is the dog damages property, and can ingest the narcotic. Something it cannot be allowed to do. It would overdose.

With the passive method the dog learns that by staring at the source of scent its toy will be thrown to it. They quickly learn to freeze, staring for ages if required at where the drugs are located. The advantages of this method is, there is little likelihood of damage to property, no damage to the drug packaging, and little to no risk of the dog ingesting drugs.

I called the CID officer over. I asked him to pull up the floorboards, while Mikey and I continued on with the search. Now its hot work for a dog searching. They get very hot. Infact they quickly can suffer nasal fatigue. Where they basically simply can't scent any more until they have had a drink and a rest. Much like us humans really! Mikey trotted off on his own. I heard slurp slurp slurp. He had found water. I followed the sound into the bathroom. He had his head down the toilet and was gulping away at the water in the pan. Not too bad, most dogs do this at some time in their lives, and in my experience always seem to know when not to do it, should there be any bleach in the water. I checked. Well, I was nearly sick. This was the filthiest speckled toilet I have ever had the displeasure to see. "Mikey" I shouted. "Out of it" he looked up at me, smiled as Labradors do when they know you are not pleased with them, and wagged his tail furiously from side to side in an unsure fashion. He then ran back into the bedroom. Come here son, I heard the CID man say. He was overjoyed as he had found a stash of brown powder under the floor. Mikey ran to him. The CID man was still on the ground. He gave Mikey a big hug. Mikey responded by licking his face all over. "I think you shouldn't let him do that" I said. "Its ok I don't mind said the officer." Come with me I said. He followed. Well, he just stood still, went a shade of grey and started retching. The householder whom was still with us thought it was tremendous. Mikey of course couldn't understand what all the fuss was about.

5 Max & the Bike Thief

Two in the morning, sitting in the police dog van eating my sandwiches, prepared earlier by my lovely wife. I just emptied the last precious drop of coffee from my flask, when I heard over the radio. "Assistance, any dog section." Two plain-clothes officers had been observing a youth in the town centre. They watched him steal a pedal cycle. Before they could grab him, he had pushed one over and ridden off on the bike. I was not far away. I sped down to the town centre to hear the youth had made for the ring road. I saw him he was coming straight at me, but on the footpath and there were heavy iron railings between us. I jumped out of the van ran to the railings which are about one meter in height and tried to grab hold of the youth. He swerved at the last second, and I grabbed at fresh air.

I called out to him, "Police Dog Section, stop or I will send the dog." I was considering how

I would do this as the railings were between us and I didn't have time to get Max over the railings sight him on the individual and send him. In the end I decided just to release Max and let him work it out. He was a veteran by this time and usually managed to do his bit best with minimum interference from me.

I opened the cage. Max had heard me shouting and knew what was required. Jumping out of the van he looked about momentarily, got his bearings, spotted the only moving target, our man. Off he went, long blond and grey wisp like hair blowing like curtains in a breeze. He was beautiful to watch. The lad on the bike made a right turn along the main route into the town centre. Max had it sorted. He ran on. I had expected he would panic and try jumping the railings. He didn't, he must have known further along there was a gap. He made for it, and turned right also, in hot pursuit. By now this youth was being watched on close circuit TV. Max was someway behind. He made good the distance. A panda (small police car), pulled up ahead of the lad. A young constable started to alight. He was quickly pulled back in by the driver. This was a friend of mine whom knew what Max was capable of when in pursuit of someone refusing to stop. Now Max had never had any input in stopping people on bikes. I didn't know what he would make of it. I didn't have to wait long. As I ran after him, puffing and wheezing I saw Max jump. What a jump. He took this lad by the right arm. The bike cartwheeled, Max went one way, the lad the other. The lad picked himself up and as Max ran towards him, he kicked Max in the side with a swinging kick. This was a mistake, Max non the worse for the kick, but enraged by it bit into the right leg of this individual, pulled and shook at the same time, dragging him onto the ground. The lad then stamped repeatedly on Max's huge head with his left foot. This caused Max to shake him like a rag doll.

"Leave," I shouted. Nevertheless, the lad continued kicking. Stand still, stop kicking him and he will let go I said. Get him off me shouted the lad, screaming. I repeated my instructions, calling on Max again to leave. This time he did. "That dogs a lunatic," exclaimed the shaken youth." I pointed out that lunatic or not, he had stopped him, and now he was under arrest on suspicion of theft. Max just stood quietly swishing his tail as if to say, "No job can beat this for job satisfaction."

6 About the Police Dog Section

Although this is essentially a book of stories concerning some of the exploits of a few of the lovely dogs I have had the pleasure of handling. I want to devote a small chapter to explaining very briefly what a police dog section does, how a potential applicant gets to be a handler, and perhaps try to clear up one or two miss conceptions that seem to abound relating to police dogs and their handlers.

The reason I came to write this book was because of the amount of times I have been asked to recount tales from my career, but I also frequently get asked such questions as;

- Does a narcotics dog have to become addicted to drugs to get it to search for them?

- Does a police dog live at the handlers' home?
- What happens to the dogs when they retire?

All questions I am asked repeatedly. I love it when people ask these questions. It shows an interest in what the police dogs do. I consider it my duty and pleasure to answer in full any questions of this nature.

Police dogs in Britain as we know and think of them have been around since the 1940s although the British Transport Police (as they are now known), were the first to employ something near to the dogs we see working today. In the early 1900s they used Airedale Terriers at Hull docks. Now all Home Office police forces and most if not all 'other' police forces have a dog section.

Police dogs are divided into different groups. The General Purpose Dog. This is what we all think of as a police dog. It is typically a German shepherd or Alsatian as once they were known. Many other breeds have been successfully used for this purpose, including; Rottwielers, Dobermans, Labradors, & Weimeranas.

GPDs as they are referred to are typically trained to perform the following tasks:

- Tracking; following a scent trail left by a

wrongdoer or perhaps a missing person.

- Searching; locating scent emanating from a person hiding in the undergrowth, or in a building. Alternatively, scent coming from lost or hidden property. Perhaps a stolen purse thrown into an overgrown area.
- Stopping a running person attempting to evade arrest by police. Not necessarily by biting! Should the person surrender the dog should "stand out," barking at the individual until the handler arrives to take charge of the situation.
- Detaining a violent or armed person whom refuses to comply with officers.
- These dogs are also taught obedience, (a must for any dog, but especially one that has been trained to bite human beings).
- Agility. It is necessary these dogs can jump fences, ditches, scramble over high walls when told to do so.

All dogs, no matter what discipline they are trained for, are taught using a reward based method. Usually a ball thrown to the dog when it successfully completes the task in hand. This is an oversimplification of the process, but this is not intended as a training manual.

All police dogs live at the homes of their handlers, and have kennels provided. If the handler is on holiday or unwell and unable to care for the dog, it is placed in the force kennels where it is looked after very well by dedicated kennel staff, which do a wonderful job.

When a dog is due to retire from service, through ill health, injury, or age, the handler usually requests to keep the dog. It will then go on to live a life as a much-loved family pet within the bosom of the family who love it. Should the handler be unable to keep the dog, a loving family from a list of people whom have shown interest in owning a retired dog, will be selected.

Narcotics and other specialist dogs: Typically, Labradors, Springer spaniels. However, as with GPDs any dog that is suitable will be considered.

To clear up the misconception that narcotic dogs are addicted to drugs in order to get them to search for them! Consider this: would it be necessary for a dog trained to search for bombs, to become addicted to bombs? Obviously not. It is no more necessary for a narcotics dog to become addicted to drugs. The same principle as for the GPDs is used. A reward based method. The dog finds the hidden drugs (or whatever it is being trained to look for), and it gets its favourite toy. Usually a ball.

Dogs for police purposes come from two main sources. Many forces breed their own dogs. Vast amounts however are donated by members of the public whom may have a dog that has become too much for them to cope with. It is typically the dogs that are considered "the head case" that make the best prospects. They are often manic because they are desperate to use their natural abilities and senses. All we do in the police service or for that matter any organisation that utilises dogs for work, is to harness their natural abilities. Dogs in the wild use their senses to survive, to find mates, to eat. Basically to hunt. All we ask of it is to do what comes naturally. If the dog struggles, or doesn't seem to be happy in its work it will be rejected and found a suitable home. Apart from being cruel to the dog, there would be no point in forcing it to work. No one wants an unwilling slave, unhappy in its work. In any case it just simply would not work to a high enough standard.

Handlers are selected from regular police constables within the force. There are only a limited number of places on a dog section. When a vacancy is likely to occur through an existing handler leaving, the position will be advertised. Interested officers can apply. If they meet the high standard required they are selected for interview. Once successful with that, they go to a dog school and are placed on a one or two week assessment known as a suitability course. The candidate with the perceived best qualities will then go onto the next available course.

Most handlers start with GPD and then having proved themselves suitable will be considered for a second, specialist dog after a couple of years.

I hope this chapter has been of interest. I have found not withstanding the amount of interest shown by the general public in the police dog sections, there is very little available in print.

7 LARGE DISTURBANCE

LARGE DISTURBANCE ANY DOG SECTION AVAILABLE? Came the call over the radio. URGENT ANY DOG UNIT?

I responded accordingly.

Go straight to The Minors arms. They are spilling out into the street fighting. Roger, on route I replied. (I am now resisting the urge not to make all the cracks as to how I knew it was Roger!!!). I was aware this pub is used extensively by members of the travelling fraternity. There had been an incident involving Town lads and a Gipsy earlier in the week. It had been quite serious. This later proved to be a result of this.

I pulled into the street. I could see no other police officers present. The urge to sit back until at least one more cop appeared was tempting, but (sound a bit cheesy) my sworn job is to protect life and property. That's the contract I entered into many years ago when I took the attestation ceremony. Anyhow I could see a young man on the ground. Everyone was fighting but I can still picture to this day what I saw. Feet stamping all over this lad. Someone else had a wooden hat stand and was smashing the base of it up and down on this lads head. I drove my van straight at them being careful not to injure the lad. I had already opened the quick release hatch on the dog cage behind my head, and Max already had his lead on. On a weekend late turn I would leave a leash on him as it was not unusual to have to get the dog out very quickly. Everyone continued fighting. These were mostly big men, not boys as one usually expects in fights of this nature. Big men with big powerful punches. Seasoned street fighters, hard men.

Max was a star. We alighted together from the drivers' door of the Astramax van. POLICE DOG SECTION I called out to make sure all my legal requirements were taken care of, as I remembered to grab the ignition keys. I pulled my truncheon from my pocket. A scene reminiscent from a film showing knights in armour must have then ensued. I wheeled my wooden club at anyone whom threatened. Max lashed out at anyone in close proximity. Between the two of us we cleared a path enabling us to protect the unconscious lad on the ground. Max pulling on the leash snarling at anyone whom came close. It seemed ages, but we were quickly joined by a handful of local officers. We eventually regained control. The unconscious lad was taken to hospital and several arrests were made. The problem in a small county force is if arrests are made, that takes officers away from the scene as they convey their prisoners. I sometimes don't think people realise how out numbered we can be in a rural force. Assistance from another town can take an age. A good dog team is worth its weight in gold in these remote areas, in circumstances such as this. Max was certainly a good dog!

8 A Training Day

Not all work required from a police dog handler is actually deploying the dog in operational scenarios. Training the dog is a hugely important aspect. Now we train our dogs to perform in a particular way. We ask for nothing less than perfection when training the animal so as to get somewhere near that perfection operationally. Of course in the real world so to speak the poor dog probably doesn't fully understand what is required of it. You see consistency is the name of the game with dog training, and operationally things can rarely be consistent.

Sometimes however even in training things don't always go to plan. We were training the dogs to search for a hidden person. They already knew the game, but what many people do not realise with dog training, it never stops. This is why people have disobedient dogs. They mistakenly believe because they have attended a dog training class, and passed with flying colours, that the dog needs no further input. WRONG, that training goes on forever. It might not need to be so regular or intense with time and age of the dog, but on it must go. Training police dogs to search for a hidden person is no exception to this.

We usually start a novice dog by letting it see a trainer run into a building holding its favourite toy. The dog runs in held back by its handler on a leash. It is upon locating the hidden person encouraged to bark. Once or twice at first, building up to a crescendo. The end result is the dog should be capable of being taken to a strange building, and tasked with searching for the scent of one or more persons hidden inside. On locating the said person the dog should alert its handler by barking continuously until joined by the handler, receiving praise/reward and terminating the exercise.

Searches, depending upon how hard the instructor makes them can take quite a long time. The dog for training purposes is encouraged to search alone, the handler staying at the entrance until alerted by the barking. Operationally one accompanies the dog for safety.

On this occasion Max was a very young police dog. We had not long since completed our basic course. The basic course for GPDs is usually about 13 weeks in duration. Max was easily at the stage of being sent into a building alone. He had enjoyed quite a few successes at work by this time. I took him to the door of the building, a large disused factory premises. The instructor gave me my briefing. One person was hidden in an inaccessible location, I had 20 minutes for the dog to locate him, and I could shout encouragement to the dog if I felt it necessary.

I sat Max by my left side, removed the lead and chain collar. POLICE DOG SECTION, COME OUT OF THE BUILDING. I challenged. Max sat quietly awaiting his release. FIND HIM I commanded. Off went Max full of drive in pursuit of his quarry. Back and forth he searched. It was a huge building. Pitter-patter I heard his huge paws padding around upstairs above us. This went on for some time, then silence. I waited. To jump in too soon with encouragement can ruin things. It sometimes takes the dog a little while to be satisfied it has located the hidden person if they are totally concealed. The dog can take a while to start to bark. Still nothing. FIND HIM Max I called out in the hopes he just needed keying in, a reminder that should he have found the hidden person that he should bark. Still nothing. No sound whatsoever.

It was no use expecting the hidden person to assist by calling out. If this person is to move the dog may take it that they are escaping and bite them.

This went on for several minutes, and then the instructor said, I think you better go and find your dog. I made my way in, being very wary. Was this a test set up by the training staff? Was I about to be jumped on by well meaning colleagues' intent on teaching me survival skills for use in the field?

I was well into the building when I heard retching noises. Very hard to hear at first, but I orientated in on them. They became louder. I was getting close to the source. An overwhelming smell hit the back of my throat causing me to retch also. I saw a cupboard, the louver door open and two old mattresses lying on the floor. The sound and the smell were coming from within. I shone my torch in to the dark space of the cupboard. There was the hidden person. Call your dog he pleaded, just call your dog. Max come I instructed wondering what the stink was. Max appeared from within the cupboard. He looked up at me swishing his thick tail as if to say, oh there you are, about time. "Get him on a lead so I can get out of here I am going to be sick," pleaded the hidden person. I obliged.

As soon as Max was on a lead, this poor person ran outside and was promptly sick. What happened in there I enquired. "Well, he found me alright," came the reply. "But as soon as he located my hiding place he managed to open the doors, he then pulled all the covers off me, climbed over the top then promptly emptied his bowels everywhere!"

I don't know whether the excitement had been too much or I had been negligent in not making sure my dog was empty prior to searching. Personally when I went back in to clean the mess up I was of the opinion Max had eaten something that definitely had disagreed with his system! It was certainly one way of getting a suspect to surrender! Tyler & the Bluff

A great deal of police work, when it comes to dealing with people is bluff. This story is no exception.

I had just finished dealing with a search for suspects when I was tasked with an attempted burglary at the other side of town. I headed across to the outskirts of a small village. There stood a lone bungalow. I spoke briefly to the lady police officer whom had attended the initial report. I was told three men had been disturbed by the owner as they had attempted to open a window to the rear of the property. When the owner had called out they had rum away. There was nothing by way of descriptions, but the fact they had run off into open countryside, and I was only fifteen minutes behind them meant it was unlikely anyone other than these people would be out there. The fact that they had run onto vegetation significantly increased the dogs' chances. Most of the searching required of us is on hard surface as we call it. This means, asphalt, concrete, tarmac, etc. This type of surface doesn't leave much in the way of scent for a dog to follow. However when people stand on grass, or other vegetation, not only do they leave their own scent behind, in the form of rafts of skin that we shed all the time. but also they crush the vegetation under foot, releasing gasses. This is very easy for a trained tracker dog to follow.

I knew this police officer quite well, and when she told me that she had not walked anywhere near the back of the house I knew she meant it. So often handlers of dogs waste time following a track that leads to a police car. Given that it is very unlikely the suspects have walked to and hidden in the police car, it is a natural suspicion that the police have been less than truthful, and have had a little nose about!

Believing what I had been told I took Police dog Tyler from the van. Tyler was about three years old. A German shepherd of huge proportions. The police service had bred him and I had looked after him from eight weeks of age. He was lovely. Big black and tan dog, with the largest darkest, most honest eyes you ever saw. He could take a big man to the ground on a training day, but refused point blank to bite anyone in real life! In every other respect he was the perfect partner to have.

I placed the tracking harness on Tyler, clipped the line to it, and off we went. He sniffed this way and that, did a double take (he never did the shakedown like Old Max had always done). Bang he was on it. Away along a grassed country lane and into a field. There was a full moon shining, it was a lovely warm still morning, probably about 3am. Nothing distracted Tyler when into a track scent. I could talk to him, but he wouldn't hear, he would just continue on like a train. I had an idea as to where we were headed (towards some old gravel pits), so for our safety I called in our location to the communications officers. In those days, Comms. officers as they are known, were older officers (like me now), who had been and done it and got the tee shirt. They had always worked the area for years and knew it like the back of their hands. Without being able to see you, they could direct you exactly.

I was mindful of the quietness. Sound carries, and every now and then I had to grab the speaker on the radio as officers on other details would call up communications. These radio transmissions can be heard for hundreds of yards on a still night in the middle of the countryside. Police radios only have a volume of loud or louder! I didn't want these individuals to hear us.

Tylers head shot up. His huge radar like ears, which always looked like they had been borrowed from a mule, waggled back and forth. He stood stock still, sniffing the air. I dropped down onto one knee, to reduce the chance of being seen. Tyler must have heard or scented someone I thought. I could hear my heart thumping; I dared not breathe less I fail to hear some sound. Then there it was, I could hear muffled voices. I cannot begin to describe the excitement one feels in moments like this. Aware you have located who you are looking for; it can still go horribly wrong. All it takes is to alert them too soon, and for them to split up and they are lost. There was no helicopter to call on in those days.

I could hear the footsteps as these people drew closer to me. I gently took hold of Tylers muzzle. He could sense the anticipation in me and was starting to squeak trembling with excitement. I was hoping they would walk virtually into me, and then I could jump up and surprise them. It would have worked, except for the dam radio. From absolute silence it crackled into action. Some PC on another detail calling up. The three men must have heard it because they started running. Initially into each other, one falling over. It would have been quite amusing had I not been trying to arrest all of them with the minimum of fuss for me. There was nothing else for it. I had to go for it. "Police with a dog," I called out into the night air. "Stand still or I will release the dog." By this time the three had sorted themselves out and were running along a hedgerow. I was trying to inform Communications of my location, but I could not give any landmarks. I called out the challenge again. This time I released Tyler to pursue. I prayed he would get hold of one should they not stop. Tyler was so reluctant to hurt people! I tried running to keep up with Tyler, but my foot went into a hole in the ground and I twisted my ankle. I got to my feet, limping but could not see any sign of the three men or Tyler. It is horrible when you lose sight of your dog when it is pursuing. The handler is there to look after the dog, and not the other way around, as so many people think. You are a team, a partnership. One cannot function without the other.

I heard a noise from my left. I went through a gap in the hedging. There I could make out three heads bobbing up and down in the moon light running further and further away from me. In normal circumstances I could easily have caught up to them. However, it is rather like when one has to fight for ones life. The adrenalin causes such fatigue so quickly. Ones legs feel full of water, heavy, almost unable to move. In reality you are moving very quickly, but this is how it seems at the time. I looked for Tyler, no sign, I was concerned. Had they injured him? I then saw the silhouette of a plant. I remember considering how like a dog sitting it looked. How like a large German shepherd, with one mule like ear forwards and the other back as if pondering what to do! I looked again, it was Tyler. What was he doing? I was running myself into a state of complete exhaustion and he was having a sit down! I challenged again. Perhaps this would cue Tyler into what he was supposed to do. Perhaps the men had not heard the challenge uttered previously and this may cause then to stop running.

Well it motivated Tyler. He jumped up from his tea break, from his senior moment, he ran past me at full tilt and after the three lads. Great I thought, he will grab one this time. I couldn't believe what I then witnessed. He ran straight up to them and turned right and sat down again. Get them I shouted, realising by now these three must know that this highly trained police dog was not going to stop them.

I was by now shattered. I had no more energy. Time to do some quick thinking. "Ok," I called out with the last remaining available breath I had in me. "Stand still, or this time I will tell the dog to bite you." I really didn't think this would work, but anything was worth arty. I knew I would never live this down if these three men all managed to evade me detaining them. I couldn't believe it! They all three threw up their hands in the air and stood still. I arrested all of them on suspicion of attempted burglary. Whilst escorting them back to the road at the point this adventure had begun I hoped they would not realise they were in no danger from Tyler, and chance another attempt at escape. They however were in awe of Tyler, complementing him on his restraint, and how they were glad they had stopped on my final warning!!! I just thought to myself, "If only they knew!"

9 Its all a Bluff!

A great deal of police work, when it comes to dealing with people is bluff. This story is no exception.

I had just finished dealing with a search for suspects when I was tasked with an attempted burglary at the other side of town. I headed across to the outskirts of a small village. There stood a lone bungalow. I spoke briefly to the lady police officer whom had attended the initial report. I was told three men had been disturbed by the owner as they had attempted to open a window to the rear of the property. When the owner had called out, they had rum away. There was nothing by way of descriptions, but the fact they had run off into open countryside, and I was only fifteen minutes behind them meant it was unlikely anyone other than these people would be out there. The fact that they had run onto vegetation significantly increased the dogs' chances. Most of the searching required of us is on hard surface as we call it. This means, asphalt, concrete, tarmac, etc. This type of surface doesn't leave much in the way of scent for a dog to follow. However when people stand on grass, or other vegetation, not only do they leave their own scent behind, in the form of rafts of skin, which we shed all the time. but also they crush the vegetation under foot, releasing gasses. This is very easy for a trained tracker dog to follow.

I knew this police officer quite well, and when she told me that she had not walked anywhere near the back of the house I knew she meant it. So often handlers of dogs waste time following a track that leads to a police car. Given that it is very unlikely, the suspects have walked to and hidden in the police car, it is a natural suspicion that the police have been less than truthful, and have had a little nose about!

Believing what I had been told I took Police dog Tyler from the van. Tyler was about three years old. A German Shepherd of huge proportions. The police service had bred him and I had looked after him from eight weeks of age. He was lovely. Big black and tan dog, with the largest darkest, most honest eyes you ever saw. He could take a big man to the ground on a training day, but refused point blank to bite anyone in real life! In every other respect he was the perfect partner to have.

I placed the tracking harness on Tyler, clipped the line to it, and off we went. He sniffed this way and that, did a double take (he never did the shakedown as Old Max had always done). Bang he was on it. Away along a grassed country lane and into a field. There was a full moon shining, it was a lovely warm still morning, probably about 3am. Nothing distracted Tyler when into a track scent. I could talk to him, but he wouldn't hear, he would just continue on like a train. I had an idea as to where we were headed (towards some old gravel pits), so for our safety I called in our location to the communications officers. In those days, Comms. Officers as they are known, were older officers (like me now), who had been and done it and got the tee shirt. They had always worked the area for years and knew it like the back of their hands. Without being able to see you, they could direct you exactly.

I was mindful of the quietness. Sound carries, and every now and then, I had to grab the speaker on the radio, as officers on other details would call up communications. These radio transmissions can be heard for hundreds of yards on a still night in the middle of the countryside. Police radios only have a volume of loud or louder! I didn't want these individuals to hear us.

Tylers head shot up. His huge radar like ears, which always looked like they had been borrowed from a mule, waggled back and forth. He stood stock still, sniffing the air. I dropped down onto one knee, to reduce the chance of being seen. Tyler must have heard or scented someone I thought. I could hear my heart thumping; I dared not breathe less I fail to hear some sound. Then there it was, I could hear muffled voices. I cannot begin to describe the excitement one feels in moments like this. Aware you have located who you are looking for; it can still go horribly wrong. All it takes is to alert them too soon, and for them to split up and they are lost. There was no helicopter to call on in those days.

I could hear the footsteps as these people drew closer to me. I gently took hold of Tylers muzzle. He could sense the anticipation in me and was starting to squeak trembling with excitement. I was hoping they would walk virtually into me, and then I could jump up and surprise them. It would have worked, except for the dam radio. From absolute silence it crackled into action. Some PC on another detail calling up. The three men must have heard it because they started running. Initially into each other, one falling over. It would have been quite amusing had I not been trying to arrest all of them with the minimum of fuss for me. There was nothing else for it. I had to go for it. "Police with a dog," I called out into the night air. "Stand still or I will release the dog." By this time the three had sorted themselves out and were running along a hedgerow. I was trying to inform Communications of my location, but I could not give any landmarks. I called out the challenge again. This time I released Tyler to pursue. I prayed he would get hold of one should they not stop. Tyler was so reluctant to hurt people! I tried running to keep up with Tyler, but my foot went into a hole in the ground and I twisted my ankle. I got to my feet, limping but could not see any sign of the three men or Tyler. It is horrible when you lose sight of your dog when it is pursuing. The handler is there to look after the dog, and not the other way around, as so many people think. You are a team, a partnership. One cannot function without the other.

I heard a noise from my left. I went through a gap in the hedging. There I could make out three heads bobbing up and down in the moon light running further and further away from me. In normal circumstances I could easily have caught up to them. However, it is rather like when one has to fight for ones life. The adrenalin causes such fatigue so quickly. Ones legs feel full of water, heavy, almost unable to move. In reality you are moving very quickly, but this is how it seems at the time. I looked for Tyler, no sign, I was concerned. Had they injured him? I then saw the silhouette of a plant. I remember considering how like a dog sitting it looked. How like a large German shepherd, with one mule like ear forwards and the other back as if pondering what to do! I looked again, it was Tyler. What was he doing? I was running myself into a state of complete exhaustion and he was having a sit down! I challenged again. Perhaps this would cue Tyler into what he was supposed to do. Perhaps the men had not heard the challenge uttered previously and this may cause then to stop running.

Well it motivated Tyler. He jumped up from his tea break, from his senior moment, he ran past me at full tilt and after the three lads. Great I thought, he will grab one this time. I couldn't believe what I then witnessed. He ran straight up to them, turned right, and sat down again. Get them I shouted, realising by now these three must know that this highly trained police dog was not going to stop them.

I was by now shattered. I had no more energy. Time to do some quick thinking. "Ok," I called out with the last remaining available breath I had in me. "Stand still, or this time I will tell the dog to bite you." I really didn't think this would work, but anything was worth arty. I knew I would never live this down if these three men all managed to evade me detaining them. I couldn't believe it! They all three threw up their hands in the air and stood still. I arrested all of them on suspicion of attempted burglary. Whilst escorting them back to the road at the point this adventure had begun I hoped they would not realise they were in no danger from Tyler, and chance another attempt at escape. They however were in awe of Tyler, complementing him on his restraint, and how they were glad they had stopped on my final warning!!! I just thought to myself, "If only they knew!"

10 "Tyler the Protector!"

How am I going to get out of this fix?" I thought to myself as I lay helplessly on the railway. I had been detailed to a reported break-in at a commercial garage on an industrial estate. Some MoT test certificated had been stolen. The premises backed onto waste ground that has a railway line running through it.

On arrival the officer dealing with the incident gave me the circumstances. Two young men had been seen breaking in. They had been challenged by the owner, and had quickly run off onto the waste ground. They had not left empty handed. Grabbing a large quantity of MoT certificates as they hurriedly left.

The conditions were excellent for a police dog to locate a scent trail. It was all vegetation which when disturbed by a hefty human foot would leave a lovely scent for the dog. There had been light rain (scent is moisture, without moisture there can be no scent), no one else in the area. It was ideal circumstances.

I prepared Police Dog Tyler for the impending search. I took him to the rear of the garage and placed the tracking harness and line on him. He wagged his tail happily. He loved tracking. Tyler was a big dog probably weighing around 100LBS. When 'on the trail' Tyler would track at a gallop. If you didn't go with him he would snatch the tracking line out of your hand. If you tried to slow him down he would loose interest. You had to go with him. Perhaps had I spent time when he was a puppy trying to slow him down it would have had some effect, but the advice always given on a training day was "run with your dog!" This naturally became what he thought was required of him when tracking. Now its all very well trainers and people who track dogs for a hobby teaching one to track at a fast pace. However when tracking 'for real' it is not such a good idea. Given that one is normally following the scent trail left by a criminal whom is intent on hiding from anyone who may dob him in, trails rarely lead over open land. They usually cross shrub land full of potholes etc. If one is running and places a foot in one of these, that is the end of things!

Anyhow, Tyler located a trail and off we went. Like a scene from Ben Hur, with horses pulling a racing chariot, so Tyler pulled me along. 100

Lbs of dog with great long legs can travel at quite a pace I can assure you. Suddenly he checked himself and retraced his steps. Sniffing at a shrub growing up the side of railway siding buildings. Oh I thought, have we found one hiding. Not a suspect, but he had located where they had hidden the MoT certificates. There they were stashed behind the shrub. I radioed up asking an officer to collect them. I praised Tyler and tasked him with continuing the track. He was soon back on it. He turned a sharp left and started heading for a local gypsy site. I knew this could mean problems. There are always dogs wandering about and that being their territory; they can be very fierce when a dog from what to them is another pack trespasses on it! I would have to deal with that when the problem presented its self.

I didn't have to dwell on that concern for long. I soon had greater worries to deal with. I could see the railway line ahead. We were approaching it at right angles. This is a small hardly used line, rust covered and overgrown by weeds, but it is used occasionally. Tyler raced up to it, and with one effortless bound, jumped over the ballast, the lines, and the cable duct coverings. Cable duct coverings are like small very thick flagstones. They are not laid in cement; they are loose, laid on top of the cables that run along the side of the lines. Because they are loose, they move. If you stand on one, it can rock or tip. I followed Tyler by jumping the lines also. My right foot just landed on the outer edge of one of these wobbly stones. Bad enough that this twisted badly my ankle, but the fact 100lbs of dog was pulling me at great speed meant things were even more sever! Crack, I heard my ankle go. I thought I had broken it. My leg would not hold me. Down I went, Tyler still pulling. I dropped the tracking line. Tyler just continued following the scent he was on. I tried to stand but the pain was intense. I fell again onto the railway. Now as I said this railway is hardly ever use. However I became aware of a rumbling clattering sound and the metal lines started to vibrate. A train was coming. I crawled off the lines. Tyler had now realised the hefty lump of meat that normally stops him going as fast as he likes was missing from the human end of the tracking line. He came back sniffing and nudging me as if to say, ok you have had a rest, now get up and lets get on with this. I stroked his big black and tan head, his huge brown eyes staring quizzically at me. I then radioed my location in to control and asked for assistance.

About quarter of an hour went by, and then I was joined by a lady sergeant. Now this is where things became even worse. No one ever considers what contingency plans to put into operation when a handler is injured. I have often enquired about it, but no one ever wants to address it (in my experience). Tyler (even though normally he wouldn't hurt anyone), saw me as injured. It was now his doggy duty to defend me. I could have done without it at this time, but it was very touching! By this time an ambulance crew had reached us. Tyler was having none of it. I told him to lie down, which he did. However he still growled and snarled whenever anyone tried to get to me. There was only one other handler on duty in the county, and he was in the middle of a detail, miles away. I asked, quite sensibly I though for my wife to be contacted. Tyler would have gone to her quite safely, he loved Sue. When I was given Tyler as a puppy I had a broken arm. Sue used to carry him about for me. It was decided to ask one of the dog handlers who lived locally but was off duty to come in and assist. He did although he did insist on receiving overtime for his efforts!

The situation then resolved. I was taken to hospital and treated. This left me with an injury I carry to present day. They told me it would have been better had I broken the ankle. I caused horrendous damage to my tendons and ligaments. Then I ended up with a severe infection in the ankle. The worst of it all was health & Safety had started to rear its head. Now I know this is for our own good, but as I was unable to return to duty my dogs were temporarily taken from me. For about four months I never saw them. They were placed in the forces kennels and incase I injured myself further I was not allowed to go and see them. I cannot bear being separated from my dogs, they are my life!

Eventually, once a doctor supported me I was allowed to go to the kennels on a weekend, and as long as I didn't take the dogs off the premises I was allowed to walk them, with the help of my wife Susan. I realise all these conditions were for my health and to protect the force from possible litigation, but at the time I was very upset!

11 Jack & the Purse

Another warm night duty, early morning, (I don't much like working the cold ones). A call to a big hotel in one of the towns within the county I police. Youths had broken into a German tour bus, left unattended outside in the hotel coach park. A quantity of miniatures and a large leather purse containing a large amount of cash stolen. I was at the other side of the county. Often I can be the only dog handler on duty and it can take ages for me to cross the county to get to details.

I arrived to find well-known and trusted officers waiting for me. They had looked about the area, but they told me exactly where they had been. They had found a dropped miniature on the grass about 20 meters from the coach. "We haven't been past where we found it," they told me. This was great help. It gives me a highly likely place to start my dog from.

This dog was PD Jack. He was a moody character. He had been a gift from a member of the public. He bit me more times than I care to remember. In the end he had a horrendous injury that wouldn't heal, and he was put to sleep. The interesting thing with Jack was he was a very loving dog, but at gone two years of age when I acquired him, I never knew what had happened to him in his previous home, to make him as handler aggressive as he could on occasions be.

Anyway, back to the story. I took Jack out of the van, tackled him up for a track and off we went. The double take and he was onto the scent. Jack was actually the finest tracking dog I handled. He tracked as well on hard surface as he did on vegetation. It made no difference to him, he loved it all. Bang, a few yards and Jack stopped. He had found a miniature. Well as we continued he must have found dozens. I couldn't pick them up, there were too many and I had to continue to try and find the cash and hopefully the suspects. We came to a high brick wall. Jack jumped over this. The trouble with walls is one never knows if the other side is the same height. It wasn't. It was three times the drop on the other side. Jack negotiated this obstacle no problem. I on the other hand, carrying everything but the proverbial kitchen sink, didn't negotiate it so smoothly! No wonder my knees are wrecked! At this point we crossed a wide main road. On the other side was a golf course. Soon we had recovered another miniature.

We were now heading for a local housing estate. We came to a river, turned right and headed for a footbridge. Over the footbridge and up to a tree. The tree had thick undergrowth all around the trunk. Grrrowl said Jack. Bark, bark, grrrowl. Jack had what's known as a hooked tail. A fault in a shepherd dog, but for our purposes it was great. When he found a hidden person, his tail would curl and uncurl like a scorpion. This was no exception. Good boy I said, tacking hold of his harness to stop him prematurely biting someone in his excitement. Come out I instructed, directing my voice towards the direction of the tree. Nothing. Come out or I will release the dog. Ok, ok, don't let the dog go pleaded a voice from deep within the undergrowth. Out came a well known youth. You are arrested for theft from the coach I said. Yeah, ok he replied. How's your dad I then enquired, not under caution. I had found him the worse for drink several days earlier and returned him to the safety of his family. Oh, he ok thanks replied the lad.

I asked the local police to attend and convey our guest to the police hotel for delinquents (the custody suit). Once this chap was safely restrained by the lady police sergeant who came to me I tasked jack with searching the undergrowth for the other lad and or further evidence. Now since I had started training Jack, the police had made improvements in forensic science. No longer do they want our dogs to retrieve found property in case it spoils forensics. We have to teach them to locate property, and indicate in the same way explosive or drugs dogs are trained. Just to stand and stair at the item. This is ok, but not much use if you cannot see the dog when it indicates that it has found something.

The above in mind. I sent Jack back in to search. A t first I thought he had found the other person. However nothing happened, jack just remained hidden in the undergrowth. All I could see was movement of nettles as he wagged his hook of a tail. Next thing he came out of the undergrowth with a large dark object in his mouth. It was the purse. Jack must have become bored waiting for me rewarding him for his find. In his frustration he must have snapped it up in his jaws and brought it to me. Better damaged forensics, than no evidence at all!

The purse still containing all the money was returned to one very happy tour guide who was very grateful to Jack.

12 Gentleman's Particulars

Sitting in a small police office on an industrial estate trying to catch up on some of the mountain of paper work one gathers in this job. It amazes me how we manage to finalise anything. For every detail one attends I guarantee you take longer writing about it than actually dealing. Especially when someone is arrested. It can take hours literally to complete the paperwork.

A call came over the local police radio. A member of the public had seen a man climbing into a junior school not far from where I was at that moment. I listened as the communications officer dispatched the detail to local officers. As a dog handler and as I get older and I believe wiser! I get quite exasperated by some of the well-meaning young officers whom attend these run of the mill details. They arrive, blue light and sirens illuminating the sky for miles around in the darkness, and sounding warning of their approach to anyone within a five-mile radius. Once on scene they alight from their cars and hunt high and low for the suspect (who has left ages ago because they heard the police well prior to their arrival). They then expect the dog unit to track the suspects down and find all the stolen property. Given that they, the officers have trampled the scene to bits, contaminating the area with their scent makes it virtually impossible for the poor dog to find anything.

My ears pricked up with this detail. No local officers were available, all dealing with prisoners in custody, or taking statements at other details. I heard the local sergeant, and a traffic officer respond. Now I knew these officers. Both are my age, and service. As one gets older and supposedly wiser one tries to deal with incidents with the least amount of physical exertion! Chasing criminals is very physically exerting! Then if you catch them and they don't want to come with you it can get very nasty. I ran to my van, jumped in and started the engine. I was quite close to the school being burgled so I quietly made my way. That's as quietly as a 2litre diesel van will let you. I called up on the radio to alert communications that I was attending, and to warn the officers attending. They responded by saying they would let me get into position on foot before they pulled up at the front of the school (so as not to spook the intruder). This is experience, and makes my job so much easier!

I pulled into the street leading to the school, accelerated hard, then cut the engine and extinguished the headlights. Usually criminals do not work alone, and any self-respecting criminal has a look out or two. I stopped the van quietly alighted, and went to the back to get my young police dog out. This dog was Elle (pronounced El, I called her Ellie). She was tiny. I recon probably the smallest working police dog in the British police service. I had handled her from being a puppy. She was bred from continental working bloodlines. Elle was the fastest thing on four legs I had ever seen. Many ridiculed her at public disorder incidents, but any that tried it on with her soon regretted it. As small as she was she had 42 perfect teeth, (20 on the top jaw and 22 on the bottom, that's what dogs have), the same as a big dog, and she knew how to use them.

I ran around the back of the school, I knew the other officers would pull up at the front. On my arrival new security fencing had been erected. This is a menace. It doesn't stop a young fit criminal probably high on some substance. It does make it difficult for a 14 stone copper, and down right dangerous for a police dog to get over. There is always a gap in it though where criminals when doing their preliminary check of the area a day or two prior to "the job," make an easy access. I found the gap, and hid in bushes to the side.

I turned the volume on my radio down as low as I could, and called the two officers. "I am in position at the back," I said. "Pull up at the front and put your blue lights on," I requested. "Is that Dave," one of them enquired. "Yes why," I responded. "Because that means Elle is there, I am not getting out came the reply." It's nice when your dog gets that reputation. Elle had a lovely nature, but when hot on the heels of a criminal, especially in the dark it was advisable not to get in her way.

The two patrol cars pulled up, quietly, but as requested lighting up the night sky. Sure enough.... CRASH (a window smashing), THUMP (a person jumping out of a window), THUD THUD THUD, (the sound of running feet on short wet grass). My heart raced, my fingers trembled with excitement (its lovely when a plan comes together). Squeal squeal said Elle, trembling with anticipation. I gently cupped her muzzle. I didn't want to have to run too far after this one. Time to act, before Mr. Burglar got into the trees. "Police Dog Section, Stand Still," I shouted with a booming voice. The lad skidded to a halt, fell over and jumped straight back up onto his feet. I repeated the challenge. He was off, as fast as he could go across the huge expanse of school playing field, towards the rear gardens of a local estate. If he gets into that I have lost him I thought to myself. I slipped the collar off Elle's neck. Stop him my girl I called to her. She was away, like she had been fired from a catapult. There was a full moon shining so I had a lovely view for Elle taking off and grabbing this lad's right arm. They crashed to the ground. Elle was only about 30kilo wet through, but the speed she moved she could take anyone off their feet. The lad struggled to slip his thick combat style coat off (Burglars dog evasion clothing). He managed, and as it came off he launched a kick at Elle hitting her on the flank. She fell back and rolled over. I was getting closer to help her. It felt like I was moving my legs but not getting anywhere. I felt helpless to protect my little girl, and he was hurting her. She bravely jumped up and went back in for another go. Bang he kicked her again. She squealed and rolled over, the wind momentarily knocked out of her little body. He turned square on (a bad decision), to prepare for another kick at Elle, I was now about ten meters away. Elle picked herself up and launched herself back at him. Crunch, she locked on right between his legs. His gentlemen's particulars were firmly gripped inside Elle's small but perfectly formed jaws!

Get it off me he screamed hysterically. Stand still I commanded. Elle LEAVE. She did. Keep that animal away from me he shouted. He went on to say, if it comes near me I will kill it. I was tempted to ask if he wanted a rematch, but I refrained!

I escorted him to the security railings. The two other cops were waiting. The lad opted to climb over (anything to place an obstacle between him and Elle). On the way over the fencing he got his foot caught in the top. He pulled it free and promptly fell on his head on the pavement. Elle stared at him, and then looked at me wagging her tail, as if to say, that will teach him.

Elle and I then checked the school grounds and recovered a computer this lad had stashed away, to return for at a later date.

The following day I had Elle checked over by a vet. She was ok. However when I went into work for night duty I learned the lad arrested had not fared so well. He admitted the burglary, and a string of other offences in interview. But had then dissolved into tears stating the dog was like a crocodile, and bemoaning the fact he had to have half a dozen staples in his nether regions!

I think he learned a valuable lesson. Not a good idea to go burglaring, but if you must and you are confronted with a police dog, no matter how small. Do not try to hurt it!

13 God Bless

As I read some of these stories to check them over, I feel I have to admit to feelings of pride and sadness. I have had the pleasure of handling some wonderful police dogs. I have kept all but one when they retired (sadly all prematurely through injury or illness). I remember the feelings I had for each one, from first seeing them, to the moment when sadly they have had to be put to sleep due to whatever ailed them. To each one of you thank you and may you rest in peace.

14 An evening with Lance

The most inconvenient aspect of police dog handling is the fact one sometimes feels a little bit trapped. Other officers from different departments finish work and have their time to themselves. As a handler one has the responsibility of the dog 24/7. Now I am sure many readers of this will be thinking, well so to does any dog owner. I assure you it's not quite the same. A privately owned dog can be cared for by a friend or relative, and if required placed in kennels whenever the need arises. A police dog is, however crude this may sound, licensed police equipment. A service dog and its handler are rigorously assessed and tested once or twice a year. More if the necessity arises. These licenses are not taken lightly. The standard expected of a police dog, whichever discipline it is from is very high indeed. No one except another qualified handler may exercise a dog owned by a police authority. Although there are force kennels with qualified kennel staff, one can not simply place a dog into the kennels without prior appointment. So when finishing work for a long weekend one has to consider that although not due into work as such, the day is not your own, you have to pop home to check on the dog and take it out. Of course none of us mind this. We agree to this responsibility when we take on the role.

There are times though when it is necessary to ask another handler to attend your home and take your dog out for you. This can be down to an unexpected delay when out for the day. Some times one has work commitments such as courses (other than dog section courses), or court appearances where one has been unable to take the dog along.

Given the nature of the work of general-purpose dogs, they are required to be assertive, and protective, it is not always a pleasant experience when asked to assist in the regard!

One of my former colleagues on the section handled a huge GSD named Lance. Lance was a comical looking dog. His ears looked like they belonged to a puppy, crossing over on top of his head. The trouble was Lance was about seven years of age! Despite this humorous look, Lance was a superb service dog, especially when it came to his assertive demeanour!

Lances handler "Jim" had decided it was time to move on career wise. He had opted for a transfer to Traffic. Jim had been given an attachment with motor patrols. He had arranged to get home to take Lance out, however due to the high volume of work he had not managed to keep this appointment.

I don't think people realise how busy the traffic department is, or what a valuable job they do in making safe our roads. Before responding to this, consider. Our roads may seem unsafe, but how much worse would they be without such officers. In addition, they are usually the first on scene at any urgent detail due to the fact they drive better-equipped vehicles than most other officer, and their driving skills are trained to a very high standard. Imagine how many serious injury accidents they deal with per shift, which could have been avoided by a modicum of care on the part of road users, and one may see why some traffic cops can seem a tad intolerant! They have my full support.

Anyhow, Jim had been delayed by an accident and was now concerned he would not get home on time, never mind just to exercise Lance. He rang me on my mobile, asking me if I would go to his house collect Lance, place him in a spare cage on the van and take him out with me for the rest of the shift. Of course I agreed, but would have preferred not to have been asked. Lance was to say the least objectionable to anyone except Jim. That's what made him a good police dog I suppose! Also the last time I had seen Lance I was assisting with his training, as the part of criminal! Further consider why most people have a dog (apart from owning it as a loving pet). It's to guard the place. It doest have to be a trained guard dog, any dog of guarding breed, of which a GSD is considered to be will do this admirably.

It was now dark, I was going to be entering Lance's garden in the dark. His kennel faced the garden gate, he was going to see me "breaking in" from the moment I clicked open the gate. I was apprehensive; Lance was going to detect this with his doggy senses the minute I arrived!

I thought of driving there very slowly. Putting off the inevitable, I thought. Better get this over with. I arrived at the house of horrors. I took my leash and chain from around my shoulder and prepared it. If held in a loop most police dogs will instinctively just put their head into the chain collar and so long as you don't do anything stupid they will be ok. I clicked the latch on the gate. The bolt was in. I had to hang over the top of the six-foot gate to open it. Lance heard and saw me. He went mad. Get it over with I decided. I marched up to his kennel and opened the door. He was snorting and snarling. Good boy I whimpered, holding out the chain in a loop. As predicted he stuck his head and ridiculous ears in it obligingly. REDICULOUS EARS!!! He must have read my thought. Oh how I wish I hadn't thought ridiculous ears!! He suddenly decided he hated me. A bite not a bad one, but bad enough if you had been me at that moment alone with this huge dog in his garden. The trouble was the chain had not gone fully over his head. As if to add insult to injury, the chain had stuck around his cars! I moved my left hand to flip the chain over the top of his head. Now a hand on top of a dominant dogs head is a threat, a show of dominance. This is why people sometimes are bitten when they reach out and touch a strange dog on the head or top of the neck. It's what dogs do when vying for top position. They Tee up, one trying to place its head over the neck of the other, and or places its paw on the neck. If one submits and allows it OK, but if both keep trying a fight may ensue. Its doggy language. Anyhow Lance objected. He showed his displeasure by biting me on the wrist. Again not a bad bite, but teeth on a bony wrist HURT! Oh dear!! I shouted in horror. Actually I didn't shout Oh dear. It was much stronger language than that. I reflected upon my choice of words as I saw Jim's neighbours peering from an upstairs window at me. What must they think of the calibre of Jim's colleagues? With that Lance bit me in the left shin. If a wrist is bony a shin is worse. If you don't believe me, try it. Anyhow I gave Jim's neighbours a further chance to hear what other colourful words I had in my vocabulary (reserved purely for occasions such as this of course)! I felt helpless. What on earth am I going to do I thought to myself. Relief, the back door to Jim's house opened. His lovely wife who was also a police officer popped her head out. What on earth are you doing she enquired quite reasonably. I humbly explained. She adjusted the collar correctly on Lance's neck. Jims Mrs. had popped home for a bite (no pun!) to eat. Had I realised she was there I would have asked her to stand with me. Lance would have accepted things had a family member been there to confirm all was alright. Think of it from his perspective. I had trespassed into his garden, broken into his kennel, shown contempt and disregard to him in his den, and tried to abduct him. We are all the same. We expect our dogs to guard our homes and families, and then we expect them to understand when we send someone in our place to look after the dog. How can they. However smart they are, they are just dogs, with doggy brains, and instincts. How many dogs injure people and are destroyed because of human (the intelligent part of the team!) ignorance?

Lance was happy now. He trotted out to the van with me and jumped in. (see if Lance had been a pet, Jims Mrs. could have walked him, but because he was a police dog, this highly trained officer had to do it!!!).

It all went swimmingly. Away from the home environment, Lance's home, his den, the place his doggy instinct tell him he must guard, he was fine. A little rumble at me when I requested he stopped sniffing someone else's poo, but otherwise he was a joy to be with.

I returned to Lanced Kingdome and knocked on the door to the house. Jims Mrs. was not in. I radioed Jim. How long will you be I asked eagerly awaiting the reply. Oh I will be ages, loads of statements to take, he said. I was nearly at the end of my shift. I had to get home as I had an appointment to keep totally unconnected with police work. Had I not I would have willingly awaited Jims late return. I dreaded going through all 'that' again, but needs must. Was I a man or a mouse (I know...squeak squeak, pass the cheese!).

I decided to do some preparations. I left Lance in the van, went into his garden, opened the kennel door, and popped some biscuit in the kennel. There were no members of the public about so I figured when I let Lance out he will be so pleased to be home, and he will smell the food and the trail of footsteps to his kennel. He will surely follow this, go in the kennel, eat the biscuit and I will shut him in. Easy. Felt very pleased with myself!

Another cursory glance about. No one in sight. Opened the van door and cage. Come on Lance, kennel I instructed bravely. He jumped out as planned. In fact it all went as planned. He munched on the biscuit joyfully. The path from gate to kennel was a long one. As I quickly made my way to lock Lance in he looked up. I am sure he had totally forgotten who I was. RAH RAH RAH he said, bouncing out on four pogo sticks, pileo erecto (hackles raised). I froze to the spot. BANG he jumped up his two front paws (actually they were fists) hitting me square in the chest. All 90lbs of him. Over I went onto my back. I covered my face with my arms like a small boy beaten to the ground by the school bully. Lance stood astride me glaring into my face his head turned to one side, looking at me with one eye, teeth on full display. He looked like the alien in that scary movie of the same name! The scene where it snarl's and salivates everywhere. "Now what," I thought. Like all 'good' dog handlers!!! I had a ball in my pocket. I did have some food in my hand but I had dropped that. In any case Lance seemed to enjoy causing me to burp in my britches in preference to eating good wholesome biscuit!

I gently rummaged into my trouser pocket. Rubber balls never want to come out with out a fight do they! When training a dog you have it all planned, as soon as he does it right I will pull out the ball and reward. The ball however has other plans; you end up dragging the entire pocket inside out due to the friction caused by rubber on cloth. Well this occasion was no exception, and Lance objected to my moving. A dog will on forcing another to submit, stand over the downed adversary until full and due homage has been paid. Usually the vanquisher will then allow the vanquished to get to its paws and go about its life uninjured. Its usually human intervention that causes any injuries. I however was not keen to await Lances acceptance, and the fact I was moving all be it involuntarily meant to him that I had not submitted! At last the dam ball came out of the pocket. I showed it to him. Small brains dogs! A BALL the must have thought, GIVE IT ME GIVE IT GO ON GIVE IT, PLEASE, PLEASE. His face said it all; this brute became a puppy in a trice! I threw the ball across the garden. Off he bounded after it. Now running isn't the advice I would give to anyone when confronted with an aggressive dog. It's possibly the worst thing one can do. However, Run I did, I scrambled to my feet and legged it, as fast as my middle-aged pins would carry me. I didn't look back, the loss of a fiver worth of rubber ball on a rope was worth it, just to escape in tact.

I got to the gate and slammed it shut. BASH, THUD, RAH RAH RAH. Lance had become a guard dog once more, remembering what he had been doing prior to this trickster producing a ball. AHA THICKO I shouted at him in relief, as I walked back to the van. I then reflected that he HAD to be left in a secure kennel, and the bolt was open on the garden gate. Well no way was I going back in, and I couldn't lean over to put the bolt in. The gate opened outwards away from the garden. I found a big stone and placed this at the foot of the gate to prevent it opening should Lance open the clasp.

I radioed Jim to let him know so he could return quickly to secure Lance.

It was past the end of my shift. I returned to my own home grateful I had only bruises where Lance had bitten me, they were more sucks than bites, but they hurt! Whilst I changed my trousers!!!! I reflected on the fact I would never ever for whatever reason agree to walk that animal again!

Not long after this ordeal, Jim was accepted onto traffic. (I would have joined traffic to had I a dog like Lance)! Lance retired and lives a life as a loved pet, yes a pet, on a remote farm. Jim visits and takes him for walks regularly. I think a remote farm is the best place for him!

15 Drunk on Duty

In this day and age any police officer found drunk on duty, or rendering themselves unfit through drink would be dismissed forthwith, and rightly so. However this member of the constabulary got away with it!

A warm autumn evening. My wife and I decided to walk the dogs an hour or two prior to me beginning night shift. We went out to the kennels to let the dogs out. When one first sees ones dogs after a break, no matter how short in duration, one should always check the dogs over. You should check for anything abnormal, look to see if they have fouled their kennel (especially if it is unusual for them to do so), and if they have one has the joyous task of examining the contense incase there is signs of foreign bodies, blood etc.

They seemed ok, with the exception of Mikey whom seemed bloated. As we walked along Sue and I both remarked how he seemed unsteady on his paws, and his eyes seemed glazed. This was not my Mikey. He was a happy bumbling Labrador retriever whom loved life so long as no one scared him; he wasn't the bravest of dogs!

We feared the worst. I always do when my dogs are unwell. I am known at work for over reacting when they seem poorly. Has he had a stroke we thought? The bloated stomach led one to believe he may be suffering the dreaded stomach bloat, or gastric torsion as it is known. This is a killer if not dealt with as soon as it is discovered, and often then it is too late. Gastric torsion is something all owners of dogs, particularly big barrel chested ones, should be aware of.

The explanation of the condition is that the disease is a mechanical twist of the stomach. The stomach, containing some reasonably heavy food substance, is pictured as swinging in a pendulum-like fashion, I think of this as a hammock rocking and then turning over, twisting the supporting cords on either end. Possibly because of the dog performing a sudden movement, the hammock, or stomach is swung completely over around the point of attachment, giving rise to a twist. This causes gases to build up, which unless released quickly by a vet will kill the dog in a most excruciatingly painful way. Warning signs seem to be many and varied however in my limited experience the dog begins to moo like a cow. This seems amusing until one realises why it is doing it! They then can bring up what resemble small bales of hay, with thick mucus. If you ever suspect this, get your dog to the vet immediately. Have someone else ring the vet as you travel. The vet will then have a fighting chance of saving your dog by being prepared. I cannot emphasize enough the seriousness of this condition.

We watched Mikey stumble about. Enough we thought. Sue grabbed the mobile phone, and rang the vet. I bundled the dogs into the cage in our estate car and off we went, a thirteen-mile journey, worrying our little friend was not going to make it. The thing was he didn't seem in pain. Sue sat in the back of the car watching him closely. "He's snoring" she said, "snoring and passing wind"! (She used another phrase for passing wind, but I am too polite to use it. I am a policeman after all!).

We arrived at the vets. We have a wonderful vet. I use the same one for my privately owned dogs as I do for the service dogs I handle. I pass several veterinary practices on route to the one I use, but a good vet is worth the time and effort. This does not mean the others are no use. However, a vet gets to know you and your dogs. This is so important when diagnosing serious problems. Find a good vet and be loyal to the practice, it is worth it I assure you.

I carried a now very round Mikey into the surgery, and plopped him on the table. The vet looked at him. A loud FAAARRRTing sound came forth, (from Mikey, not the vet). Everyone sniggered. A moment of light relief in this moment of terror. The vet pinched Mikey skin (to ascertain if he was dehydrated, the skin stays nipped together if it is); he then shone a light into Mikey big brown eyes. They were drawn and glassy. The vet whom I knew well. Looked at us in that all knowing way. Like he had something to say, but didn't know how to tell you. Oh no I thought. This is it; he is going to have to put my little boy to sleep. I could feel myself welling up as I do when these sad times come calling. "He's drunk" said the vet. I looked at him in relief and disbelief at the same time. "What?" I retorted, "He's drunk," came the reply. How I enquired. Have you got fruit trees enquired the vet. My brother, whose land we adjoin has an ancient orchard. Yes I said sheepishly. "I recon he's been eating the rotten windfall," said the vet. "It will have fermented and turned to alcohol."

Naturally Sue and I were very relieved. I left the vets feeling a little ashamed at my lack of knowledge; however I had now added that to my list of things I know about dogs. I have always been fascinated by dogs, dog behaviour, and dog training. My earliest recollection of this interest is from when I was five years old. I remember being dragged around the paddock at home (where I still reside), by my mums golden retriever. I vividly remember trying to bribe it with digestive biscuits, to jump small hurdles intended for a small pony that lived in our field. I love learning all I can, and get great joy from passing that knowledge on to others, that it may help them with their dogs. The point of this book, although hopefully an enjoyable light-hearted insight into police dogs and their handler. Is to drop in useful pointers to help dog enthusiasts along the way. I do hope it does so!

We arrived home, just in time for me to begin my night duty. I bundled the German shepherd into the dog van. Better leave Mikey at home I thought, drunken bum!

I completed my shift and eight hours later arrived home. Mikey stood in his kennel looking eagerly at me, wagging his tail from side to side furiously causing his entire body to move about. I wanted sleep. Oh how I wanted sleep. Mikey however wanted play and amusement. No hangover there! Perhaps I shall resort to eating rotten fruit instead of drinking beer. Whenever I have overindulged I get a blinding headache!

I was just pleased he was well. My little Mikey was back.

16 Decency repaid in full

If I can refer you to the story in chapter 2. I concluded by mentioning meeting the two lads I arrested on another occasion.

I am a great believer in you reap what you sow. What goes around comes around, and all that! This story shows how true this belief is.

Communications were trying in vane to get a free officer to attend a report of youths causing annoyance to residents in a small street in town.

I know how frustrating it can be when trying to sleep during the early hours and some idiot in the street thinks they have to shout and wake the entire street. If you go out to ask them to tone it down, they can get nasty. Even if nothing happens to you, they may return and damage your home. This can go on for ages ruining your life, for what! This is what the police are for, dealing with these everyday annoying life destroying incidents, which plague some unfortunate peoples lives on a regular basis. Nuisance can be more serious than many crimes. Crimes for many of us as private clean living citizens are fortunately infrequent. Nuisance however taunts us all. Even coppers when off duty.

I shouted up on the radio. "I'm free," (sounding like Mr. Humphries from the TV comedy "are you being served"). Thanks Dave, came the reply. Everyone else is tied up. Not a problem I enthusiastically replied. I carefully drove the half mile to the detail. This was a run of the mill job. No signs of urgency. No need to drive quickly or use the warning instruments on the van. The amount of people whom think police or other emergency staff use the blue lights incorrectly is amazes me. Do people really think that any 'sensible' person in the emergency services would do this? Every detail is logged. If we learn of a detail first hand and communications are unaware, we call it in to log it before speeding to it. Of course in all walks of life there are good and bad and the emergency services are no exception, but overall we are just everyday ordinary people whom choose a job where we can be of use to the public. Anyhow, even though trained to do it, driving quickly is stressful. As a police officer one is expected to be a highly trained driver, know the roads as well as a London cabbie, be a lawyer, a self-defence expert, and marriage guidance councillor. The list goes on. A lot is expected, and the more one has to do, the more chance of error creeps in!

I arrived at the street in question. About twenty young men were gathered. They were very angry about something. Well I knew there was no one else to help me, so I called in just so communications knew what I was up against, incase I needed urgent assistance.

It was no good getting the dog out to clear them. On your own with a crowd, all that happens is they surround you and the dog. There are times when you do it, if someone needs help and serious injury would be likely to a member of the public, but it's a risk. On this occasion these men were just making a noise. No need to make worse the situation. I should however have left my drivers door window open, and the quick release hatch open on the van, so Max could get to me should I need him to. I didn't. I just alighted from the van and went to talk to these people. It was about 3am on a Saturday morning. "Come on lads" I said "keep it down a bit, people are trying to sleep." That was all I said. The situation however erupted immediately. Abuse too strong to show in a nice little book such as this was directed at me. In a trice I was engulphed in a crowd of angry young me. "Kick the .... Out of him, he on his own" I heard someone say. I was terrified, but hopefully didn't show it. In a rural county force as small as the one I serve in, you meet the same people repeatedly, on and off duty. One can never ever back down. You could never do your job with any authority if you did. The lads you regularly deal with have to know this, or they would always try to intimidate you, at home or at work!

This is it I thought, pressing the radio button in the hope communications might hear I was in trouble. This is it, another beating. I have had a few in my time that have left me classed as slightly disabled. I actually do receive a small disability allowance from a beating I received off duty trying to help a lad being beaten up by two other men.

Then someone spoke up. "Leave him, he is ok. They moved towards me still very hostile. LEAVE HIM ALONE HE IS OK. DON'T TOUCH HIM. Why said one of the crowd. This bit is so vividly left in my mind. He got me and Joe one day with his dog. He could have put the dog on us. One of the coppers wanted him to, but he wouldn't, he's ok. It was one of the lads from the track along the river, when they swam to the other side and I got them with the help pf Max to swim back to me.

They all wandered off, quiet as mice. I nodded in appreciation to this lad, whom I have met again several times.

What you do in this life returns to you, when you least expect it to. If you treat people as you wish to be treated, it can be a positive welcome return!

17 What goes in must come out

I was on a narcotics dog course. We were at our police headquarters. It is not just police that receive training at our police dog school. Members of the prison service also train with us. On this particular day I was up for annual relicensing & assessment. Four prison officers were with me and about to be assessed by their own assessor from the prison service. I was talking to this assessor. I had Mikey on a lead by my side, as I was awaiting a call to go and conduct my search in order to qualify. The prison assessor, whom was nothing to do with my examination, was opening his packed lunch, which consisted of sandwiched wrapped in Clingfilm. Both he and I should have known better. We must have had over forty year's professional dog handling experience between us. He lowered his hands, holding the sandwiches tantalisingly before Mickey's nose. He fiddled to undo the Clingfilm that always refuses to give up its contents without a fight. "Ouch! You sod" I heard this man exclaim. Mikey had snatched the entire pack, still encased in plastic wrapping. The fact it was so wrapped must have helped it slide down faster than normal, as when I attempted to open his jaws to remove the sandwiches from within, all had gone without trace. The only evidence, repeated licking of his doggy lips with delight.

Everyone laughed, and I just made a mental note of when it happened so as if any signs of ill health should appear I could get him treatment. He is a Labrador, and has eaten worse than Clingfilm, to no determent!

I can't really remember how long passed. A day or two perhaps.

I was on duty, and decided to let my two dogs out of the van for a wee stop. They ran about playing as they always did. Then I saw Mikey stop for a poo. I watched so as I could go, poo bag in hand and gather up this parcel. Have you noticed? Poos move. You can memorise their exact location, but by the time you get to them they have relocated! This was no exception. I hunted about. Success, I found it, stooped down and picked up the warm steaming substance in the poo bag.

I looked up (its moments like this when you take your eyes off your dogs for a second, when they get themselves into all kinds of trouble. What on earth is he doing I thought to myself. Mikey was scampering about in fits and starts. He was unhappy; I could see this from his body language. He was hunched up, running about, stopping checking his rear-end studiously, dragging the wheelbarrow as I put it. That's dragging his bottom along the ground, his hind legs straight out in front of him, pulling for all his might with his forepaws. Then around and around the field we were in, scampering as fast as he could go. I called him in so as I could see what was ailing him. He ignored me so enthralled with his posterior was he! Then I noticed a slightly brown, translucent membrane like thing hanging out of his bottom. My god, he's passing the lining of his innards I thought panic stricken!

I called him in successfully this time. To my relief, it was the Clingfilm he enjoyed a day or two before when he stole the sandwiches. I put on my medical gloves (I can touch anything as long as I have them on my hands), and gently pulled it from his nether regions.

I looked around to make sure no one had seen. I realise this is nothing really, but I was in full uniform at the time. Have you noticed you are always on your own when something embarrassing occurs, but someone always arrives just before you get away with it? I think dogs organise things this way. How can we embarrass him today I always imagine they think to them selves! This was no exception. A party of schoolchildren had been walking past with their teacher, when they spotted us. Oh let us watch the policeman training his dogs they must have thought! It seemed to amuse them anyway. I took a bow, put the Clingfilm and gloves in a dog waste bin, and introduced the dogs to the children.

Printed in the United Kingdom
by Lightning Source UK Ltd.
121324UK00001B/14/A